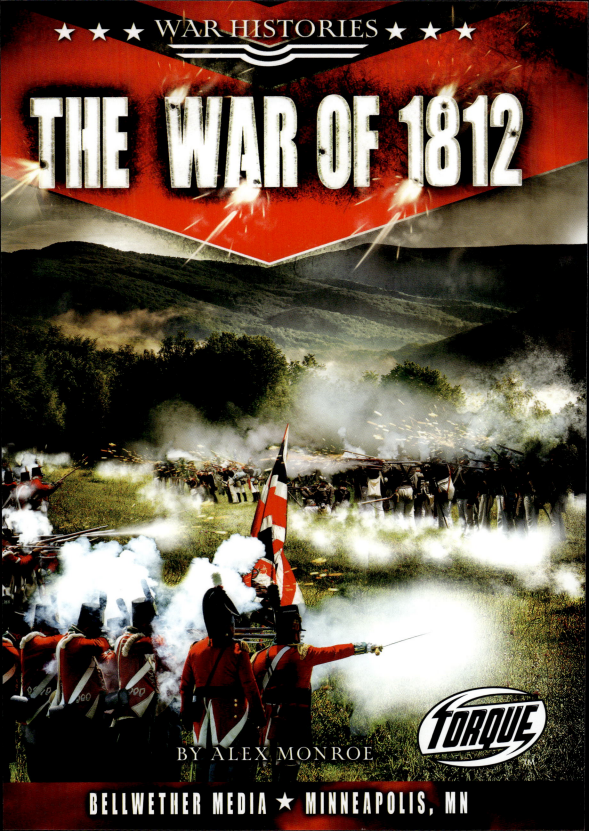

Torque brims with excitement perfect for thrill-seekers of all kinds. Discover daring survival skills, explore uncharted worlds, and marvel at mighty engines and extreme sports. In *Torque* books, anything can happen. Are you ready?

This edition first published in 2025 by Bellwether Media, Inc.

No part of this publication may be reproduced in whole or in part without written permission of the publisher. For information regarding permission, write to Bellwether Media, Inc., Attention: Permissions Department, 6012 Blue Circle Drive, Minnetonka, MN 55343.

Library of Congress Cataloging-in-Publication Data

Names: Monroe, Alex (Writer of children's books), author.
Title: The War of 1812 / by Alex Monroe.
Description: Minneapolis, MN : Bellwether Media, 2025. | Series: Torque: War Histories | Includes bibliographical references and index. | Audience: Ages 7-12 | Audience: Grades 4-6 | Summary: "Engaging images accompany information about the War of 1812. The combination of high-interest subject matter and light text is intended for students in grades 3 through 7"– Provided by publisher.
Identifiers: LCCN 2024035378 (print) | LCCN 2024035379 (ebook) | ISBN 9798893042740 (library binding) | ISBN 9798893044188 (paperback) | ISBN 9798893043716 (ebook)
Subjects: LCSH: United States–History–War of 1812–Juvenile literature.
Classification: LCC E354 .M58 2025 (print) | LCC E354 (ebook) | DDC 973.5/2–dc23/eng/20240801
LC record available at https://lccn.loc.gov/2024035378
LC ebook record available at https://lccn.loc.gov/2024035379

Text copyright © 2025 by Bellwether Media, Inc. TORQUE and associated logos are trademarks and/or registered trademarks of Bellwether Media, Inc.

Editor: Rebecca Sabelko   Designer: Josh Brink

Printed in the United States of America, North Mankato, MN.

TABLE OF CONTENTS

WHAT WAS THE WAR OF 1812?	4
FIGHTING NEAR AND FAR	6
MR. MADISON'S WAR	8
BRITISH INVASION	16
ALL TIED UP	18
GLOSSARY	22
TO LEARN MORE	23
INDEX	24

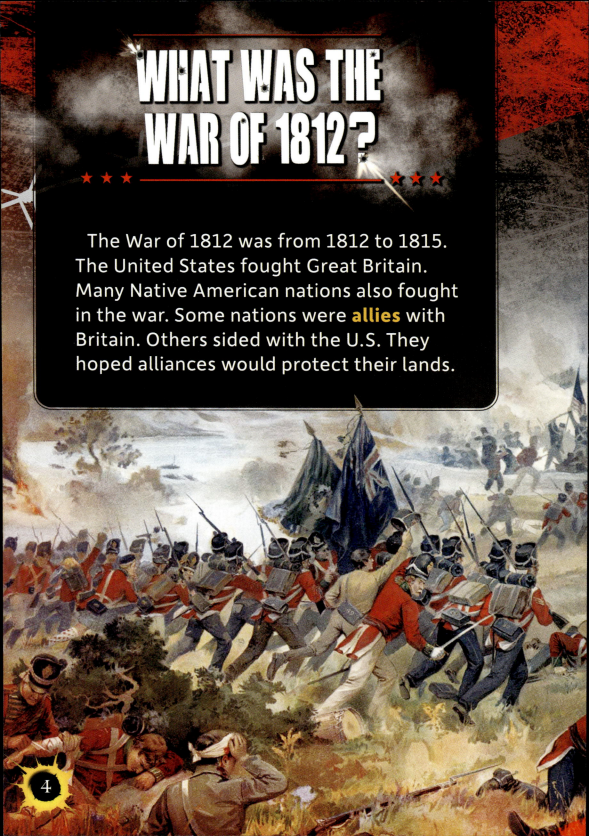

WHAT WAS THE WAR OF 1812?

The War of 1812 was from 1812 to 1815. The United States fought Great Britain. Many Native American nations also fought in the war. Some nations were **allies** with Britain. Others sided with the U.S. They hoped alliances would protect their lands.

FIGHTING NEAR AND FAR

In the early 1800s, Britain and France were at war. Britain made **blockades** to stop any trade with France. This hurt U.S. trade. Britain also **impressed** U.S. sailors.

PAINTING OF A BATTLE BETWEEN BRITAIN AND FRANCE

PAINTING OF A SHAWNEE VILLAGE BEFORE U.S. SETTLEMENT

Meanwhile, Native American nations were fighting U.S. **settlers**. They were protecting their lands. The U.S. thought Britain was helping Native Americans. **Tensions** grew.

MR. MADISON'S WAR

In 1812, U.S. President James Madison asked **Congress** to declare war against Britain. The vote passed. On June 18, the War of 1812 started.

BY ANOTHER NAME

The War of 1812 is often called Mr. Madison's War. It is named after President James Madison.

BATTLE OF QUEENSTON HEIGHTS

U.S. LEADER

NAME
James Madison

NATIONALITY
American

RANK
U.S. President (1809 to 1817)

IMPORTANT ACTIONS
- 1812: Asked to declare war
- 1814: Supported troops after the Battle of Bladensburg
- 1815: Signed the Treaty of Ghent

  The first major battle was the Battle of Queenston Heights. The U.S. tried to **invade** Canada. Canada was controlled by Britain. The U.S. hoped taking over Canada would quickly end the war. But the U.S. lost the battle.

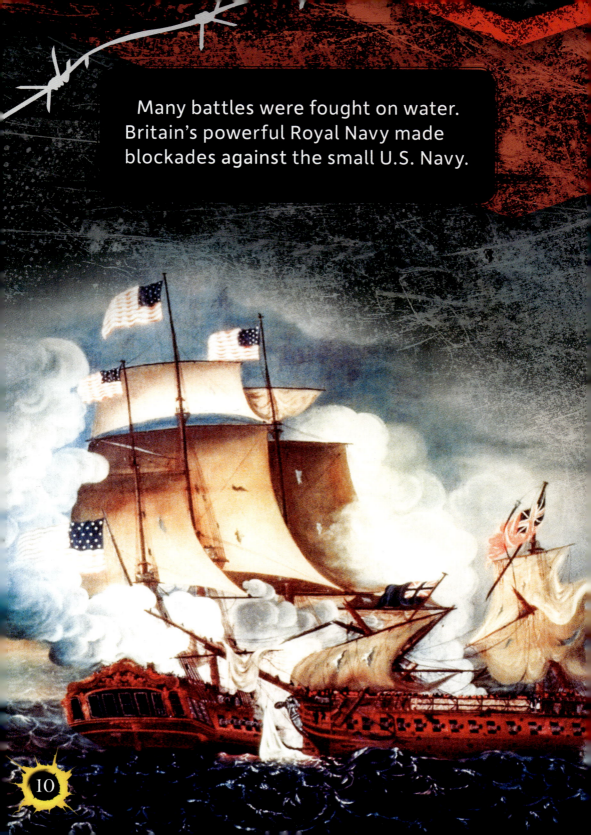

Many battles were fought on water. Britain's powerful Royal Navy made blockades against the small U.S. Navy.

★ WAR OF 1812 SHIPS ★

HMS *SHANNON*

Type	Used By	Size
frigate	Royal Navy	more than 150 feet (45.7 meters) long

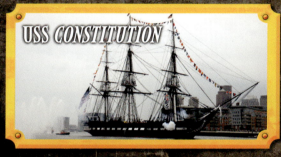
USS *CONSTITUTION*

Type	Used By	Size
frigate	U.S. Navy	204 feet (62.2 meters) long

Both sides fought on **frigates** and **sloops**. Frigates were large. They had many cannons. They were used in battles. Sloops were small and fast. They were often used by **privateers** to capture enemy supplies.

The U.S. won major battles in 1813. In September, the U.S. won the Battle of Lake Erie. They forced British troops to **retreat** into Canada.

In October, the U.S. defeated British and Native American forces in the Battle of the Thames. Chief Tecumseh died in the battle. He led an alliance of Native American nations. This alliance broke apart when he died.

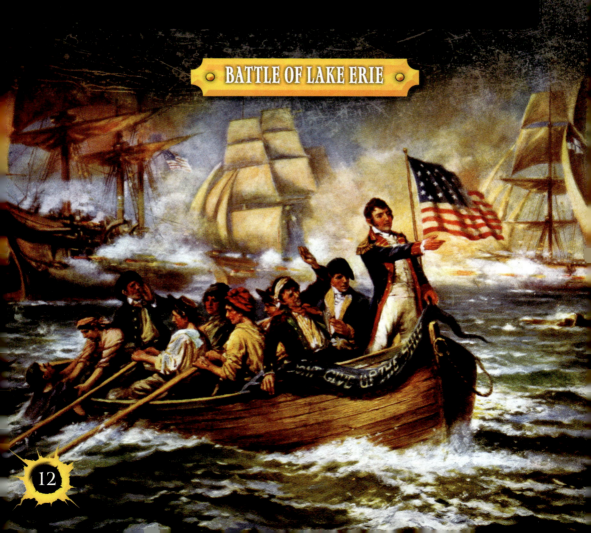

BATTLE OF LAKE ERIE

BATTLE OF LAKE ERIE MAP

British fleet =
American fleet =

Lake Erie

TECUMSEH

Tecumseh was a Shawnee chief. He was a skilled leader. He tried to protect Native American lands from settlers.

Support for the war was split. Some British people were against it because Britain was also at war with France. Supporters wanted to stop the trade relationship between the U.S. and France.

In the U.S., some people feared the war would hurt trade. Others hoped the war would help the U.S. grow westward.

PAINTING OF FOOD SUPPLIED TO U.S. TROOPS

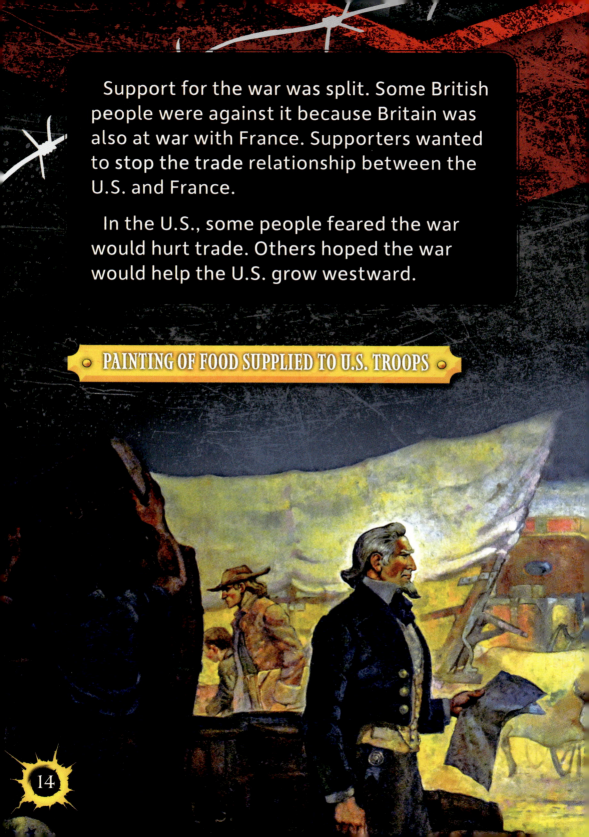

THE WAR AT HOME

Women took on new roles during the war. They ran farms and businesses.

Women also directly helped soldiers. They cooked at camps. They tended to hurt soldiers. They sewed U.S. flags. Some women sent important information to military officials.

BRITISH INVASION

In 1814, Britain defeated France. More troops could fight in the U.S. On August 24, British leader Robert Ross and his soldiers won the Battle of Bladensburg. He ordered troops to burn much of Washington, D.C.

In September, Britain tried to capture Baltimore, Maryland. The city was important for the U.S. Navy. The U.S. won the Battle of Baltimore. Britain retreated.

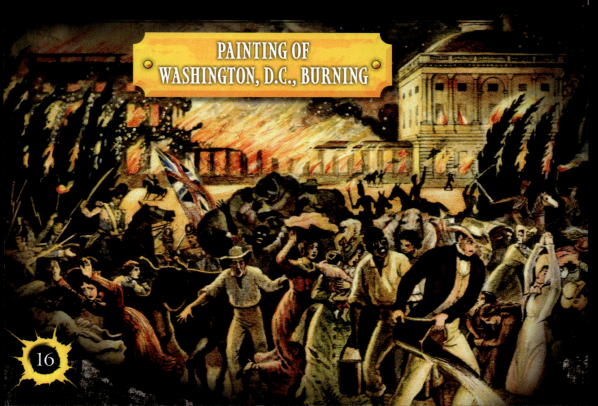

PAINTING OF WASHINGTON, D.C., BURNING

★ BRITISH LEADER ★

NAME
Robert Ross

NATIONALITY
British

RANK
British Major General

IMPORTANT ACTIONS
- August 1814: Led Britain to win the Battle of Bladensburg

- August 1814: Ordered the burning of the White House, the U.S. Capitol building, and more

- September 1814: Died during the Battle of Baltimore

THE STAR-SPANGLED BANNER

Francis Scott Key wrote "The Star-Spangled Banner" during the Battle of Baltimore. It later became the U.S. national anthem.

ALL TIED UP

Both sides struggled to win the war. In December 1814, U.S. and British leaders signed the **Treaty** of Ghent. Any captured land would be returned to its original owners.

On February 17, 1815, the War of 1812 officially ended. It was a tie.

THE WAR OF 1812 TIMELINE

June 18, 1812
The U.S. declares war on Great Britain

October 13, 1812
The U.S. loses the Battle of Queenston Heights

October 5, 1813
Chief Tecumseh dies in the Battle of the Thames

TREATY OF GHENT

August 24, 1814 — British troops burn down Washington, D.C.

January 8, 1815 — The U.S. wins the Battle of New Orleans

February 17, 1815 — The War of 1812 officially ends

19

The War of 1812 caused great loss for Native Americans. They lost great leaders. Their lands were taken. They faced more hardships as the U.S. expanded westward.

The war did not end impressment or the blockades that caused the war. These ended soon after Britain defeated France. Today, the U.S. and Britain are strong allies.

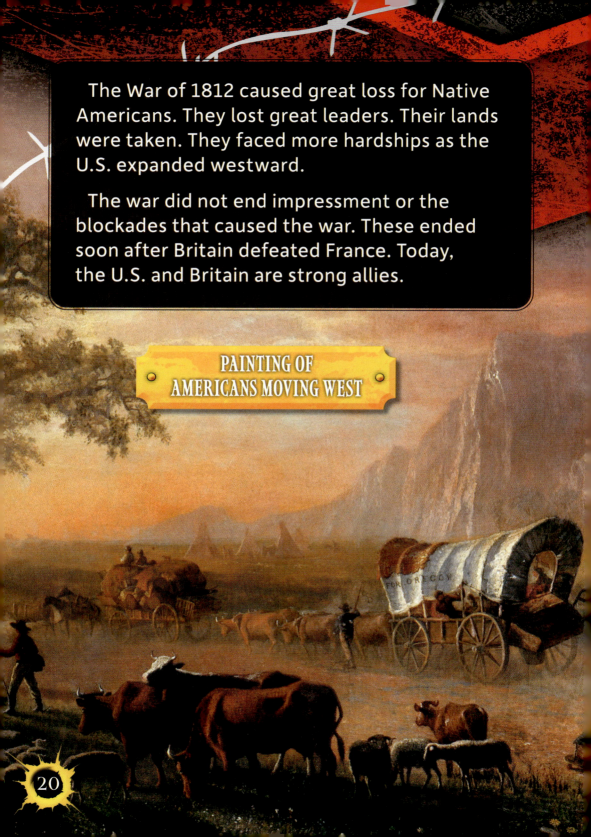

PAINTING OF AMERICANS MOVING WEST

BY THE NUMBERS

1,000 people = 👤

NATIONS INVOLVED

- Great Britain, many Native American nations and First Nations, United States

ESTIMATED NUMBER OF DEATHS IN BATTLE

- U.S.: around **2,260** 👤👤
- Great Britain: around **2,000** 👤👤
- Native Americans (British allies): around **1,000** 👤

NUMBER OF U.S. MILITARY PERSONNEL

- **286,730**

ESTIMATED COST OF THE WAR OF 1812 TO THE U.S.

- more than **$3.2 billion** (in 2024 dollars)

NUMBER OF WARSHIPS IN 1812

- U.S.: **15**
- Great Britain: **600**

GLOSSARY

allies—countries that support and help other countries in a war

blockades—groups of ships used to seal off areas, such as harbors, to prevent people and goods from leaving or coming into the areas

Congress—the group of people that makes laws for the United States

frigates—large ships used in war

impressed—forced into naval service

invade—to enter a land to control it

privateers—sailors on ships who are licensed to attack enemy ships

retreat—to withdraw troops away from an enemy

settlers—people who move to live in a new region

sloops—sailboats with single masts

tensions—states of being in which people or countries disagree with or feel anger toward each other

treaty—an agreement between two countries

TO LEARN MORE

AT THE LIBRARY

Doeden, Matt. *Taking A Stand During the War of 1812: An Interactive Look at History*. North Mankato, Minn.: Capstone, 2023.

Gunderson, Megan M. *James Madison*. Minneapolis, Minn.: Abdo Publishing, 2021.

Sonneborn, Liz. *The Shawnee*. Minneapolis, Minn.: Bellwether Media, 2024.

ON THE WEB

Factsurfer.com gives you a safe, fun way to find more information.

1. Go to www.factsurfer.com

2. Enter "War of 1812" into the search box and click 🔍.

3. Select your book cover to see a list of related content.

INDEX

allies, 4, 12, 20
Battle of Baltimore, 16, 17
Battle of Bladensburg, 16
Battle of Lake Erie, 12, 13
Battle of Queenston Heights, 8, 9
Battle of the Thames, 12
blockades, 6, 10, 20
by the numbers, 21
Canada, 5, 9, 12
Chief Tecumseh, 12, 13
Congress, 8
France, 6, 14, 16, 20
frigates, 11
Great Britain, 4, 6, 7, 8, 9, 10, 12, 14, 16, 18, 20
impressed, 6, 20
Key, Francis Scott, 17
lands, 4, 7, 13, 18, 20
leaders, 9, 17
Madison, James, 8, 9
map, 5, 13
name, 8
Native American nations, 4, 7, 12, 13, 20
navies, 10, 16
privateers, 11
Ross, Robert, 16, 17
settlers, 7, 13
sloops, 11
timeline, 18–19
trade, 5, 6, 14
Treaty of Ghent, 18, 19
troops, 12, 14, 16
United States, 4, 5, 6, 7, 8, 9, 12, 14, 16, 17, 18, 20
war at home, 15
Washington, D.C., 16

The images in this book are reproduced through the courtesy of: David P. Lewis, front cover (British soldiers front bottom left); J.T. Lewis, front cover (British soldiers middle bottom left); TrishZ, front cover (British soldiers top left); Peter K. Burian/ Wiki Commons, front cover (British soldier with flag); Photawa, front cover (American soldier front); Wally Stemberger, front cover (American soldiers middle); John Prior/ Wiki Commons, front cover (American soldiers middle end); New Orleans Museum of Art/ Wiki Commons, pp. 2-3, 22-24; Library & Archives Canada/ John David Kelly/ Wiki Commons, pp. 4-5; National Maritime Museum, Greenwich, London/ Wiki Commons, pp. 6-7; Angel Wynn, p. 7; James B. Dennis/ Wiki Commons, pp. 8-9; The White House Historical Association/ John Vanderlyn/ Wiki Commons, p. 9; Bettmann/ Getty Images, pp. 10, 16-17; Edward Pritchard/ Wiki Commons, p. 11 (HMS *Shannon*); Seaman Matthew R. Fairchild/ Wiki Commons, p. 11 (USS *Constitution*); Photo12 / Ann Ronan Picture Library/ Alamy, pp. 12-13; steeve-x-art/ Alamy, p. 13; Albany Times Union/ Hearst Newspapers/ Getty Images, pp. 14-15; Virtue, Emmins & Co./ Wiki Commons, p. 15; Spellcast/ Wiki Commons, p. 17; Scorpius59/ Wiki Commons, p. 18 (October 13, 1812); Charles Phelps Cushing/ Alamy, p. 18 (October 5, 1813); Heritage Images/ Getty Images, pp. 18-19; Library of Congress/ Wiki Commons, p. 19 (August 24, 1814); Kurz & Allison/ Wiki Commons, p. 19 (January 8, 1815); Photo Researchers/ Alamy, pp. 20-21.